My Alphabet Bible Story Book

All Rights Reserved

No part of this book may be reproduced or copied in any form or by any means, electronic, mechanical, photocopying, recording or by any information storage or retrieval system without prior written permission of the Publisher. Inquiries should be addressed to the name and address below.

Thank you.
Published By:
Million Words Publishing, LLC
Enjoyed By You!
WORDS THAT LAST FOREVER!®
www.millionwordspublishing.com

Library of Congress Catalog Card Number: 2017902777

ISBN-10: 1-891282-09-3
ISBN-13: 978-1-891282-09-6

My Alphabet Bible Story Book
Illustrated By: Renea Robinson

© 2016

My Alphabet Bible Story Book

Written & Illustrated By: Renea Robinson

This book is dedicated to All God's precious children around the world! Know that you are All God's chosen! Jesus loves you!

A is for...

Adam

B is for...
BIBLE

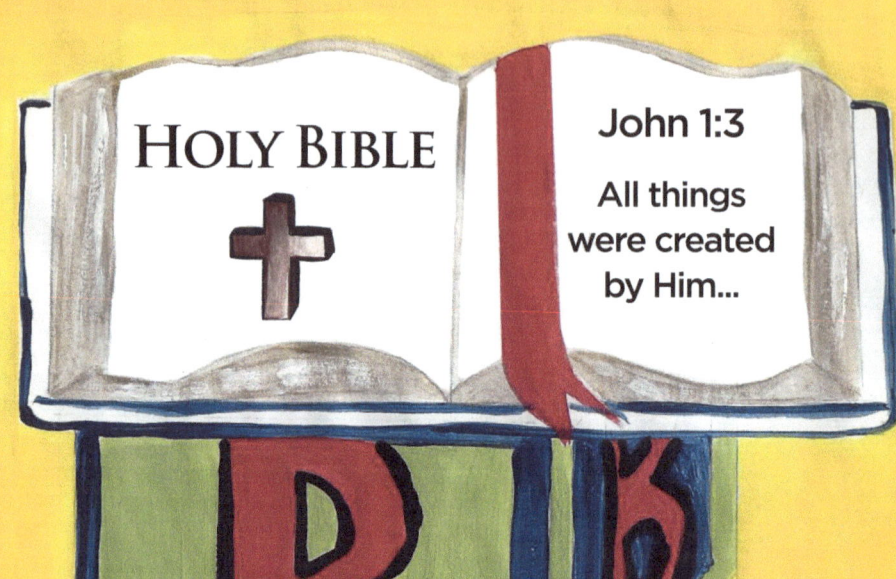

Bible

C is for...

Church
A place for Praise and Worship

D is for...

Old Testament
Genesis
Exodus
Leviticus
Numbers
Deuteronomy
Joshua
Judges
Ruth
1 Samuel
2 Samuel
1 Kings
2 Kings
1 Chronicles
2 Chronicles

Deuteronomy

E is for...

Esther

Faithful God Forever

G is for...

Glorious

H is for...

HOLY

I is for...

Isaiah
The 23rd book of the Bible

J is for...

Jesus

K is for...

King

L is for...

Loving God

Loving God is He

M is for...

Moses

N is for...

Naomi

O is for...

Obedient
The way that we should be

P is for...

prayer

Q is for...

Queen Athaliah

(A-tha-li-ah)

R is for...

Rainbow
The promise God made to us

S is for...

Savior

T is for...

Timothy

U is for...

Uzziah
who became King of Judah. (Uz-zi-ah)

V is for...

Virtuous

W is for...

Wisdom

X is for...

xerxes
ZlXerx-esl a King found in Esther

Y is for...

Young Child, and Z is for Zion

NOW I KNOW MORE FROM THE BIBLE!

www.ingramcontent.com/pod-product-compliance
Lightning Source LLC
Chambersburg PA
CBHW042251100526
44587CB00002B/93